BCS
IT Security

Level 1

using Windows XP/Vista

Release BCS007v1

Published by:

> CiA Training Ltd
> Business & Innovation Centre
> Sunderland Enterprise Park
> Sunderland SR5 2TH
> United Kingdom

> Tel: +44 (0) 191 549 5002
> Fax: +44 (0) 191 549 9005

> E-mail: info@ciatraining.co.uk
> Web: www.ciatraining.co.uk

ISBN 13: 978 1 86005 822 6

First published 2009

Aims

To make the user aware of security risks associated with computer use, both at work and at home, and to familiarise the user with ways of protecting against such risks.

Objectives

After completing the guide the user will be able to:

- Be aware of the threats made to systems performance and how to protect against those threats

- Understand the importance of information security and how to protect that information

- Be aware of risks associated with network use, Bluetooth and portable devices and understand the measures taken to protect against them

- Understand the importance of following the guidelines and procedures for the secure use of IT

- Be aware of the risks to data security and know how to prevent them.

Assessment of Knowledge

At the end of this guide is a section called the **Record of Achievement Matrix**. Before the guide is started it is recommended that the user complete the matrix to measure the level of current knowledge.

Tick boxes are provided for each feature. 1 is for no knowledge, 2 some knowledge and 3 is for competent.

After working through a section, complete the **Record of Achievement** matrix for that section and only when competent in all areas move on to the next section.

Contents

Section 1
Security Awareness

By the end of this Section you should be able to:

Appreciate the Security Risks involved in using IT

Understand Threats associated with E-mail

Be Able to Identify Unwanted and Hoax Messages

Be Aware of Viruses and other Threats to your PC

To gain an understanding of the above features, work through the **Exercises** in this **Section**.

For each **Exercise**, read the **Guidelines**, without touching the keyboard, then work through the numbered steps of the **Actions** on the computer. Complete the **Revision Exercise(s)** at the end of the section to test your knowledge.

Exercise 1 - Awareness

Guidelines

A life without computers would be hard to imagine today. They are used in almost every walk of life and the majority of people will use a computer at home and possibly at work too.

Although computers can make our lives so much easier, you must be aware of the security implications of using them. Steps must be taken to protect your computer hardware, systems and portable devices, your personal information and data and you must follow guidelines relating to IT security and privacy of information. You must respect the confidentiality of information that you have access to. All organisations should have a privacy policy to show you how to do this. They should also have an e-mail and Internet use policy and health and safety guidelines to follow. Make sure you know where to find the relevant guidelines and procedures for your organisation and make sure you follow them. Find out who to approach if you have any questions relating to the laws and guidelines governing the safe use of IT, or who to contact if you need to report a security concern.

The Internet and e-mail are useful tools for accessing information and communicating, but it's essential to be aware of the risk of attack from other users with hostile intent. This guide will try to explain the dangers and to help you avoid the pitfalls.

Actions

Food for thought...

1. Think about your computer use at home. What do you use it for?

2. Do you think you are reasonably aware of security issues?

3. Do you consider your computer adequately protected?

4. Do you use a computer where you work or study?

5. Do you feel that you have any responsibility for the security of the data on this computer?

Exercise 2 - E-mail Basics

Guidelines

Today, e-mail is an extremely important business tool and many businesses would, almost, come to a standstill without it. It has obvious advantages over the normal postal system: it is much faster - mail is delivered within seconds. Rather than pay excessive postage for sending paper copies of files through the post or by courier, electronic files can be attached to e-mail messages. All the sender pays is the cost of a local telephone call with a dial up connection, or a lot less if they have a broadband connection. Consider how much more quickly business documents can be sent overseas using e-mail than by using surface or airmail. A point of note is that some anti-virus software/firewalls prevent certain types of attachment, which contain macros (such as databases) passing through. This is because some viruses use macros to work.

Before using e-mail, familiarise yourself with the rules of **netiquette** - network etiquette. Always use accurate and brief subjects in the appropriate field on a message. Keep your messages brief and relevant rather than rambling. Ask before sending large attachments; don't send heated messages (flames); don't use all UPPERCASE – it is the same as shouting; when replying, always make sure the subject is still relevant to your reply.

Make sure your outgoing messages are spelled correctly, just as you would before sending a letter. Many e-mail programs allow you to format messages with different colours, fonts and backgrounds. This provides an opportunity to show some individuality.

Consider the implications very carefully before sending any sensitive information by e-mail. In a work situation, you must familiarise yourself with the e-mail policy in place. Usually, common business rules and regulations state that you must not send messages that might offend, or jokes, etc. Never send "chain letters". Basically only subject matter directly associated with the business should be sent via e-mail.

Actions

1. Why does some anti-virus software prevent file attachments containing macros from getting through?

2. What is the name for the etiquette that should be followed when using e-mail?

3. At work, what type of e-mails should be sent?

Exercise 3 - Unwanted & Hoax Messages

Guidelines

Unwanted messages

Be prepared to receive unwanted e-mails. Certain companies and individuals send out masses of junk mail (spam).

Any message, whether received via e-mail or through the door, which promises riches, prizes, or rewards in return for a cash payment or supplying your bank/credit card details should be regarded with the suspicion it deserves and be deleted or thrown away immediately.

Some more subtle tricks have included official-looking e-mails supposedly from banks, etc., asking you to confirm card details and/or PIN numbers. This is known as **phishing**. Delete them. Banks will never ask for such information to be put in an e-mail.

Be very careful who you give personal information to – identity theft is also a risk with e-mail. Take as much care to protect your privacy while using e-mail as you would in shredding normal mail before putting it in the bin.

Be suspicious of all e-mails from unknown sources. If in doubt, it is a good idea to get a second opinion. Preferably ask someone with experience of Internet and e-mail matters and whose opinion you trust.

i *These topics are covered in further detail in the following exercises: 5, 8 and 12.*

Hoax messages

Hoax e-mails, such as chain messages or bogus petitions, are at best a nuisance, but they can be used to collect e-mail addresses and some are more ominous. These e-mails usually take a particular format, such as fake virus warnings, offers of cash if you forward the message, appeals to help a sick person, chain e-mails, which you must forward to a specified number of people for good luck. Spammers often use these e-mails to collect addresses; they can then send out a vast amount of spam e-mails, which appear to originate from your address.

There are some clues that can help you spot a hoax. Some examples are: requests to forward a message to lots of people (sometimes to everyone you know); unsupported claims that many other people have won prizes or cash; naming a legitimate company, e.g. Sainsbury's, who will give you a £50 voucher if you forward this to 20 friends; language used in a way to create a sense of urgency, e.g. "act now to protect your computer from this devastating virus", or "send money now" to pay for medical care for someone at death's door.

If you receive a message that you are afraid may be a hoax, delete it. Do not, under any circumstance, forward it to anyone else.

Exercise 4 - Viruses

Guidelines

A computer **virus** is a piece of malicious software code introduced to a computer system, with the ability to spread itself to other computers. This should not be confused with the term bug, which describes an error or fault in a piece of software code. The extent of the harm caused by viruses varies enormously.

In many cases the contamination remains unnoticed in its host file until a specific event triggers off its action. Viruses can cause many levels of harm to a computer system. The least harmful might cause slightly odd things to happen to a file, for example if a user typed text into a word processed document on an infected computer, certain letters or words might appear on screen in an unexpected text format. Another result of a relatively harmless virus could be the refusal of an application to save files to any area other than a specific folder on the hard disk drive, rather than the desired folder. The action that a virus carries out when activated is known as the **payload**.

At the other end of the scale, a virus might lie dormant until the built in clock within a PC reaches a certain time on a certain date, or possibly until the computer has been restarted a certain number of times, and then become active. This type of virus is variously known as a time bomb or logic bomb. It could then destroy the entire file structure on the hard disk drive and make the drive completely useless. If this type of virus infected a network, the effect could be catastrophic.

Macro viruses are those that are added to executable files within an application. The most common of these can occur within the template files in *Microsoft Word* and *Excel*. This is why you are sometimes given the option of opening such a file with macros disabled. If the macro can't run, neither can any virus that might be within it!

Be vigilant about e-mail messages; they can contain viruses. Ensure you have up to date anti-virus software installed on your computer. Messages without a subject or from an unknown source should be treated with caution. Save attached files to disk and scan them before opening if you are at all suspicious. If you do open a message attachment that contains a virus, the results can be disastrous for your computer.

Exercise 4 - Continued

A common type of virus is one that arrives in an e-mail attachment, installs itself within the recipient's *Outlook* or **Contacts** address book and automatically e-mails itself to some or all of the e-mail addresses it finds there. These viruses are particularly effective since the recipient may not realise that the virus has arrived, or they have spread the infection onwards. The new victims are less likely to be suspicious of attachments e-mailed to them by a known contact.

Viruses can <u>only</u> become active within a system if they are introduced to the system from outside and then activated.

The only pathways available to viruses are via input devices such as floppy disks, memory sticks, CDs or DVDs or the Internet. If only genuine application software from reputable sources is installed on a PC, in theory there should be no danger. If, however, disks containing applications or files are borrowed or bought from dubious or unknown sources, the chance of them containing viruses is much greater.

As mentioned earlier, e-mails received with file attachments are a major source of viruses and should be treated with particular caution, as should any files downloaded from the Internet that have a **.exe** extension. This extension identifies executable files, i.e. files that are actual programs that will open up and run. If the file contains a virus, the virus will run with the program!

Actions

1. What is a computer **virus**?

2. What is the name for the action carried out by a virus when it is activated?

3. What is the name for a virus that may lie dormant until a certain date and time?

4. What is a common way for a virus to get into your computer?

5. Which type of file should you be very careful about downloading from the Internet?

Exercise 5 - Other Threats

Guidelines

Worms and Trojans

A **worm** is a self replicating computer program, which uses a computer network to send copies of itself within a system to other computers on the network. It's not a virus, but can open a door for a virus to enter. At best, it simply clogs up the system resources.

A **Trojan** is **malware** (a malicious program) and its name comes from the story of the Trojan horse, because it is disguised as a link to a file that a user would be particularly tempted to open, e.g. a game or a graphics file. Once the link is opened, the Trojan gains access to the system.

Adware, Spyware and Rogue Diallers

Adware is any software package which automatically plays, displays, or downloads advertisements to a computer after the software is installed on it or while the application is being used. Some types of adware are also spyware.

Spyware is software that is installed without the user's knowledge on their computer to interfere with their interaction with the computer. This is done without their knowledge. These programs can gather personal information, such as Internet browsing history, can redirect your browser and can install additional software. Spyware can change computer settings, interfere with Internet browsing, slow down your connection and can sometimes result in loss of a functioning Internet connection or of other programs.

A **rogue dialler** is a piece of software which is installed on your computer without your knowledge, usually when you open a spam e-mail or visit a website which contains hidden malicious software. It affects dial up connections by deleting the internet service provider's phone number and replacing it with a premium rate number.

This means that each time you connect to the Internet you are running up a massive phone bill. If you have broadband instead of dial-up Internet access you should not be affected, as broadband connections work in a different way and cannot be changed by rogue dialler software.

Exercise 5 - Continued

Hacking

The term **hacking** basically means changing computer software (or hardware) to do something other than what it was intended to do. It can be used to gain access to systems thought to be secure in order to access or steal data on them.

However, hacking can sometimes be constructive. Many "hackers" are expert programmers and some companies or organisations employ them to find any flaws in their security system, so they can then repair them.

Actions

1. What is a **worm**?

2. What is **spyware**?

3. What is the name for software that deletes a legitimate dial up connection and instead dials premium rate numbers?

4. Which type of Internet connection will not be affected by the software referred to in question 3?

Exercise 6 - Revision

This Exercise covers the features introduced in this section. Try not to refer to the previous Exercises while completing it.

1. Why shouldn't you send an e-mail that has been typed in capital letters?

2. What is another name for **junk e-mail**?

3. What should you do if you receive an e-mail from an unknown source?

4. List some examples of the form hoax e-mails can take.

5. What should you do with a message you think may be a hoax?

6. Is a **bug** the same as a **virus**?

7. List the pathways to your computer that are available to a virus.

8. What is the name for software disguised as a link to a file that someone would be tempted to open?

9. What is **adware**?

10. What does **hacking** mean?

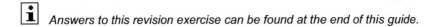 *Answers to this revision exercise can be found at the end of this guide.*

If you experienced any difficulty completing this Revision, refer back to the Exercises in this section. Then redo the Revision.

Once you are confident with the features, complete the Record of Achievement Matrix referring to the section, at the end of the guide. Only when competent move on to the next Section.

Section 2
Protecting your PC

By the end of this Section you should be able to:

Know Which Anti-virus Measures can be Taken

Understand how Anti-virus Software Works

To gain an understanding of the above features, work through the **Exercises** in this **Section**.

For each **Exercise**, read the **Guidelines**, without touching the keyboard, then work through the numbered steps of the **Actions** on the computer. Complete the **Revision Exercise(s)** at the end of the section to test your knowledge.

Exercise 7 - Security Measures

Guidelines

Basic security measures

Taking certain basic safety precautions will reduce the chances of suffering a security breach of your computer:

- Ensure a firewall is installed and running (see below).
- Keep your computer secure with the latest software updates by running Windows Update regularly.
- Install reliable anti-virus software and keep it updated.
- Install reliable anti-spyware software and keep it updated.
- Use the anti-virus and anti-spyware software to carry out regular scans of the <u>entire</u> system.
- Use the software to scan any removable disk that is placed in a drive on the system before installing or opening any files from it.
- Be conscious about the source of any software you use!
- Save any files downloaded from the Internet to the hard disk drive and scan them with anti-virus software <u>before</u> opening them.
- Be particularly suspicious of any e-mail messages containing attachments from an unknown source.
- Even be suspicious of any e-mail messages from a known source!
- Always virus-scan everything that you download from the internet or receive by email!

Firewall

Every computer should have an operational firewall. A firewall is effectively a filter that determines what type of traffic is allowed to pass out of the system to the Internet, and into the system from the Internet. It helps to protect the computer from the risk of infiltration.

Actions

1. What should you do before installing or opening files from a removable disk?

2. What protection should every computer have?

Exercise 8 - Anti-Threat Software

Guidelines

Anti-virus software

Every computer system in use should have an anti-virus program installed. It is important to be aware of the limitations of anti-virus software. Virus writers modify existing viruses and create new examples almost every day. This means that the writers of AV software must modify their own software on almost a daily basis, in order to maintain the effectiveness of their products. Once you have installed an AV program it should be updated immediately since it will have been sitting in stock for a number of weeks. Updating is typically done via the Internet and

normally you can specify how and when it takes place. At the specified time the software will access the Internet, check for current update files, download them and automatically install the new data files. This procedure should be carried out on at least a weekly basis, to ensure that effective AV protection is maintained. An AV program, purchased and installed 18 months previously and never updated, is virtually useless!

Once an AV program has been installed, configured and updated, it must be used conscientiously, i.e. used regularly to scan the entire contents of the computer and set up to automatically scan any incoming e-mails and Internet downloads.

If an AV program detects the presence of a virus during a scan, one of two courses of action should be followed:

The file containing the virus should be disinfected. This means that the elements of malicious programming within the file are identified and deleted, leaving the file in its original, harmless state. An effective AV program will give the user the option of allowing it to do this.

If an AV program detects a virus that it does not recognise, i.e. a virus that has been created too recently for the AV updates to disinfect, the software should offer to quarantine the infected file. This means that the AV software will move the infected file into a protected folder within its own installation. From this quarantine area, the entire file can either be uploaded to the AV software supplier's web site for their attention, or simply deleted by the user so that it presents no further threat.

Exercise 8 - Continued

If, in spite of taking all the recommended precautions, a system does become infected, the appropriate staff member should be informed, the computer affected should be removed from any network connection and disinfected in the manner described above. If this is not effective, specialist IT support should be sought.

Anti-Spyware Software

As with anti-virus software, all computer users should install and run anti-spyware software to protect their systems. Anti-spyware programs prevent spyware and adware from being installed on your computer, and keep your computer and your personal information secure. Microsoft offer the free Windows Defender for this purpose.

Again, new spyware and adware is released every day! Be vigilant - keep your anti-spyware software up-to-date by installing the latest updates and perform a full scan of your computer regularly.

Anti-Spam Software

Spam mails are a used by many companies as a way of advertising, as it is relatively easy to do. We all get e-mails about medicines, car insurance, etc. However, apart from being annoying, spam mails can be a way of introducing viruses to your computer. Anti-spam software is an effective way of filtering these unwanted messages and is often included with your anti-virus software.

Actions

1. What should you do immediately after installing anti-virus software?

2. Why?

3. How often should you update the software generally?

4. What action should you take if a computer system does become infected?

Exercise 9 - Revision

This Exercise covers the features introduced in this section. Try not to refer to the previous Exercises while completing it.

1. What is a **firewall**?

2. You only have to update anti-virus software immediately after installation. True or false?

3. What should you regularly use the anti-virus program for?

4. What can an AV program do it it comes across a virus it doesn't recognise?

5. What can be used to deal with unwanted spam mail?

Answers to this revision exercise can be found at the end of this guide.

If you experienced any difficulty completing this exercise, refer back to the Exercises in this section. Then redo the Revision Exercise.

Once you are confident with the features, complete the Record of Achievement Matrix referring to the section at the end of the guide. Only when competent move on to the next Section.

Section 3
Information Security

By the end of this Section you should be able to:

Appreciate Privacy Issues

Change a Password

Understand Threats to the Security of Information

To gain an understanding of the above features, work through the **Exercises** in this **Section**.

For each **Exercise**, read the **Guidelines**, without touching the keyboard, then work through the numbered steps of the **Actions** on the computer. Complete the **Revision Exercise(s)** at the end of the section to test your knowledge.

Exercise 10 - Privacy Issues

Guidelines

Passwords and PINs

If the content of certain files is considered to be sensitive or confidential, password protection should be used to prevent unauthorised persons accessing, viewing or editing the data. A password typically acts as a user's personal entry code to their own PC, software or files and would usually be chosen by the user and never divulged to anyone.

A perfect password will consist of a combination of letters and numbers and be of an adequate length, e.g. 8 characters, not just 3. Don't use something too simple like your name, date of birth or your dog's name. You should never share a password, or for that matter a PIN number, with another person and never write it down. Passwords should be changed regularly, to prevent the possibility of misuse by unauthorised individuals.

As well as password protection, most organisations or systems require the use of a **user ID** (a user-name or log-in name). This is another level of access code that provides evidence of a user's entitlement to access certain areas of a network or system. A user ID would typically be assigned to users by the relevant organisation, i.e. the owner/administrator of the system or network in question. A number of users might be given the same user ID. This would identify to the system the fact that the user could legitimately claim access to the network; also, it would identify the level of access to which the user was entitled. The password would also be necessary to identify the individual user, and provide evidence of their entitlement to access their own files, within an area of the network designated as "theirs". See information on authentication, identification and authorisation later in this exercise.

Access Rights

The different levels of access given by different user IDs are known as **access rights**. It is important that organisations have security policies in place with regard to access rights, in order that only appropriate personnel have access to the system and only appropriate personnel have access to sensitive parts of the system. These security precautions should be taken on top of normal, sensible physical security measures such as burglar alarms, locks and keys, etc.

Exercise 10 - Continued

Logging On Checks

There are three processes that are activated when a user logs on to a computer system: **authentication, identification** and **authorisation**. Authentication is simply the process to find out if someone is who they are saying they are, i.e. on computer networks authentication is carried out by checking log on user passwords. The process of identification connects the information you have given in your user name and password and checks that it matches the details held for you. Once you've been authenticated and identified, then the authorisation process checks if you have the required permissions to access the content. This is a bit like the computer saying, "I know who you are, now I'm checking what you're allowed to do".

Actions

1.   Which of the following examples is the best password:

     a) d86yhp19?

     b) freddy?

     c) 12349876?

2.   Give 2 alternative names for a **user ID**.

3.   What are the different levels of access allowed by different user IDs known as?

4.   Name the 3 processes that are activated by a user logging on to a computer system.

Exercise 11 - Changing a Password

Guidelines

It is good practice to change your password or PIN number regularly to keep your PC secure; sometimes you might have to change it if security has been breached.

The process usually follows a similar pattern; you log on using your old password, select to change it, when you will be requested to enter your old password/PIN, then enter your new one, then confirm the new one.

Actions

 This exercise refers to computers on a network or at home that require a log on password to start them. If your computer works without entering a password to log on then read this exercise for information.

1. As an example, to change your *Windows* log on password, click **Start** and then **Control Panel**.

2. Select the **User Accounts** link.

 *If you're viewing the **Classic View** of **Control Panel**, double-click on the **User Accounts** icon.*

3. In the **User Accounts** window, select your user name.

4. Choose the **Change your password** link.

5. In the first text box, enter your existing password.

6. In the next two text boxes, enter the password you would like to start using. Entering the password twice helps to make sure that you typed your new password correctly.

7. Click **Change Password** to confirm the changes.

8. Close the **User Accounts** window.

9. Close the **Control Panel** window. From now on you need to use your new password to log on, after re-starting the computer.

Exercise 12 - Information Security

Guidelines

You must ensure that you do not disclose information inappropriately, whether it is personal information, or relating to someone else. Even if you are careful, it's a sad fact that there are people who will try to steal sensitive information from computer users and Internet browsers. Be aware!

Phishing

The process of attempting to gain sensitive information such as user names, passwords and credit card details by masquerading as a trustworthy organisation, usually in an e-mail. If you receive an official-looking e-mail supposedly from a bank, etc., asking you to confirm card details and/or PIN numbers, delete it. Banks will never ask for such information to be put in an e-mail. Be suspicious of all e-mails from unknown sources, especially those with attachments. If in doubt, it is a good idea to get a second opinion. Preferably ask someone with experience of Internet/e-mail matters and whose opinion you trust. Phishing is a way of committing identity theft.

Identity Theft

Identity theft is the fraudulent use of your personal details by criminals. They steal this information and use it to commit crimes, such as opening a bank account or applying for credit cards, in your name. They can obtain documents such as passports and driving licences in this way. Your identity is your property and very important, so you must take steps to protect it.

Actions

1. What should you do if you receive an e-mail, which looks like it comes from your bank, asking you to confirm your account number, sort code and telephone banking password?

2. What might a criminal use your personal details to do?

Exercise 13 - Revision

This Exercise covers the features introduced in this section. Try not to refer to the previous Exercises while completing it.

1. If files are confidential or sensitive, what should be used to prevent any unauthorised person from accessing them?

2. What should you do/not do to protect your password or PIN number?

3. What is **authentication**?

4. Which process checks your access permissions?

5. What should you regularly do with a password or PIN?

6. What is the name for the practice of trying to obtain personal information by pretending to be a legitimate organisation?

7. What is the term used for the fraudulent use of other peoples' personal details by criminals?

i *Answers to this revision exercise can be found at the end of this guide.*

If you experienced any difficulty completing the Revision, refer back to the Exercises in this section. Then redo the Revision.

Once you are confident with the features, complete the Record of Achievement Matrix referring to the section at the end of the guide. Only when competent move on to the next Section.

Section 4
Technology Security

By the end of this Section you should be able to:

Understand how to Physically Protect IT Devices

Know how to Keep Data Safe

Understand Safety Measures for Networks

Know about Network Passwords and Security Settings

To gain an understanding of the above features, work through the **Exercises** in this **Section**.

For each **Exercise**, read the **Guidelines**, without touching the keyboard, then work through the numbered steps of the **Actions** on the computer. Complete the **Revision Exercise(s)** at the end of the section to test your knowledge.

Exercise 14 - Physical Measures

Guidelines

Security of Hardware

Thieves don't just need a password to get at your data - they might sometimes take the PC itself! If you don't have a highly secure office, it may be worth investing in cables to lock your computer, monitor, printers, etc. to the furniture. It's much more difficult to steal a desk than an unsecured computer.

Security of Portable Devices

Portable devices are particularly vulnerable to loss or theft, because of their size and, of course, portability. Take especial care of laptops, PDAs (personal digital assistants, e.g. BlackBerry), notebooks, mobile phones, multimedia players, e.g. iPod. Although you can lock these devices, it doesn't stop you losing them, or them being taken by someone.

Be security conscious - never leave devices visible in a car. You also need to take care of removable storage devices, such as USB memory sticks or cards, especially if they contain sensitive, confidential or valuable information. Basically, make sure that all portable devices and removable devices are stored in a safe and secure way.

Actions

1. What can you buy to physically secure IT equipment?

2. Why are portable devices especially attractive to thieves?

Exercise 15 - Keeping Data Safe

Guidelines

Backing Up

Certain parts of a PC's memory are only temporary; it is, therefore, good practice to save your work to permanent storage (hard disk drive or file server) after regular, short periods. This ensures that if a power cut occurs, only the data produced since the last save is lost. Certain software applications perform this task automatically. Sometimes, if something goes wrong and power is lost while you are using a file, that data may become corrupted. If you've made regular saves, you'll be able to go back to the most recent one and rescue most of the data.

Apart from protecting data against loss due to power failure, an organisation needs to consider the possibility of total file loss due to: a serious hardware fault, physical damage to the computer (possibly as a result of fire), infection by computer virus, theft or other malicious action, or by accidental deletion.

The loss of vital files may be inconvenient to an individual using a home PC for hobby purposes, but to a business user, large or small, the loss could well be catastrophic. This means it's essential to make regular, complete copies of all files that are identified as being critical to an organisation. This is known as **backing up** files and may be carried out hourly, daily, weekly or whenever is considered necessary. Regular backing up ensures that even in the event of a total loss of data, an organisation has an almost current, duplicate set of its most important files, which it can rely upon to maintain business continuity.

Storage containing the backed up material is known as **backing store** and should be treated as a very valuable commodity. The fundamental reason for backing up files is to ensure that they cannot be lost, or completely destroyed, while saved on the hard drive of the PC or the file server. This means that it's not totally secure to keep the backing store in the same room, or even the same building, as the source material because of the risk of fire.

For absolute security, the backing store should be removed from the working environment (off site) and more than one set of backing store media should be used in rotation. All backup media should be kept in a storage environment, which is theft-proof, fireproof and waterproof.

For an individual home PC user, such sophisticated techniques are unnecessary; however some backing up should be carried out. Always try to bear in mind how much time and effort would be lost if your PC either switched itself off or blew up! If the former happened, you would lose all unsaved work, if the latter, you would lose all work saved on your hard disk drive as well as all application software installed on your machine.

Exercise 15 - Continued

Storage

Make sure all important personal data you use is safely stored. For example, have a copy on the hard drive of your computer and a backup on a CD, or on a memory stick.

It is highly likely that at some point, for whatever reason, you will need to re-install application software. It is also good practice to keep all the original media on which application software is supplied, i.e. program CDs or floppies, in a secure place, away from any risk of damage or theft.

Security of Data

If you need to leave your computer unattended for any reason, make sure you lock it, or log off. This will prevent anyone accessing your data while you are away.

Actions

1. Why should you back up data?

2. Should you keep the backed up data in the office?

3. Is it necessary to back up data on a home computer?

4. How should you store application software media?

Exercise 16 - Network & Wireless Safety

Guidelines

Computers that are connected to each other create a network and these are often set up with public IP (**Internet Protocol**) addresses. This means that the computers on the public network can be seen by computers outside the network, i.e. from another network, or the Internet. If a network is set up as private, computers outside the network cannot see them. Computers on a public network have no barriers between themselves and all the other computers on the Internet. This visibility can make a computer network vulnerable to attack if it is not properly secured.

Wireless Networks

If you work on a wireless network, you must understand that it too needs to be secured to prevent other wireless network users accessing it. In the diagram below, a computer is connected to a wireless network (**freebox**). Notice that another wireless connection (**Livebox-9842**) is within range. However, as both networks are secured by encrypted passwords, neither can access the other.

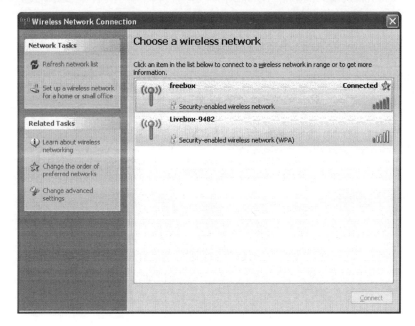

Exercise 16 - Continued

Encryption

Any information on an unsecured network will be visible to others. If you know that the network you are using is not secure, do not send any confidential information across it, unless the data is encrypted. Cryptography is the practice of hiding information. Encryption is the process of scrambling data into a form that can't be easily understood by anyone not authorised to access it. It works around the principle of a key locking (encrypting) the data and another key unlocking (decrypting) it.

Connectivity

Bluetooth connectivity is a way of connecting various devices, e.g. computers, phones, multimedia devices, and is wireless and automatic. The range between Bluetooth devices is about 10 metres and up to 8 devices can be connected at the same time. Because of the wireless connection, you need to take precautions to make sure the signals aren't intercepted.

Bluetooth users can set up trusted devices that can exchange data without asking permission. When any other device tries to establish a connection to a device, the user has to decide to allow it. Alternatively the device may be switched to non-discoverable mode and then will not connect with any other Bluetooth devices.

Actions

1. What makes a public network vulnerable?

2. What must be done to a wireless network to prevent other wireless users accessing it?

3. What is **encryption**?

4. What type of connectivity does Bluetooth use?

Exercise 17 - Passwords & Security Settings

Guidelines

For security reasons, it is good practice to use your own passwords and settings on networks, individual computers and programs, rather than the default, or pre-existing ones. If a password is already in use, then it follows that someone else knows it. See *Privacy Issues Exercise 10* for advice on setting and using passwords. Internet security settings can also be adjusted to prevent other Internet users from accessing your network.

Actions

1. To change Internet security settings, in *Internet Explorer*, select **Tools | Internet Options** and the **Security** tab.

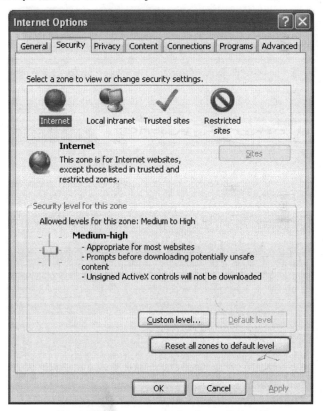

This example shows a screenshot from Internet Explorer 7

2. Make any adjustments required and then click **OK**.

Exercise 18 - Revision

This Exercise covers the features introduced in this section. Try not to refer to the previous Exercises while completing it.

1.   What is the name for the process of copying data to another location and storing it securely called?

2.   How often should this process be carried out?

3.   What type of storage environment should backup media be kept in?

4.   What is the term for a group of computers connected to each other?

5.   What is the difference between a private and a public network?

6.   What connectivity is a way of connecting various devices, automatically?

7.   Is it good practice to use default network passwords?

Answers to this revision exercise can be found at the end of this guide.

If you experienced any difficulty completing the Revision, refer back to the Exercises in this section. Then redo the Revision.

Once you are confident with the features, complete the Record of Achievement Matrix referring to the section at the end of the guide.

Answers

Please note: these are example answers only.

Exercise 2

Step 1   Some viruses use macros to work, so anti-virus software may prevent them from getting through.

Step 2   Netiquette.

Step 3   Only subject matter directly associated with the business should be sent.

Exercise 4

Step 1   A computer virus is malicious software code that gets into a PC and can cause damage.

Step 2   The payload.

Step 3   A time bomb, or logic bomb.

Step 4   Via an e-mail attachment.

Step 5   Be very careful about downloading a file with a **.exe** extension.

Exercise 5

Step 1   A worm is a computer program that copies itself within a system to other computers on a network.

Step 2   Spyware is software installed without a user's knowledge and interferes with their interaction with their computer.

Step 3   A rogue dialler.

Step 4   Broadband connections are not affected by rogue dialler software.

Exercise 6

Step 1   Because it's the same as shouting.

Step 2   Spam.

Step 3   Ask for a second opinion - is it legitimate?

Step 4   Chain e-mails, petitions, false virus warning, cash offers, appeals for help.

Step 5   Delete it.

Step 6   No, a bug is an error in software code and a virus is malicious software code.

Exercise 6 - Continued

Step 7   Input devices - floppy disks, CD/DVDs, memory sticks, or the Internet.

Step 8   A Trojan.

Step 9   Software that automatically plays, displays or downloads adverts to a computer.

Step 10   Changing software to do something other than what it was originally intended to do.

Exercise 7

Step 1   Use anti-virus software to scan the removable disk.

Step 2   Every computer should have an operational firewall.

Exercise 8

Step 1   You should update an anti-virus program immediately after installation.

Step 2   Because new viruses appear daily and it could have been on a shelf for some time.

Step 3   At least weekly.

Step 4   Tell the appropriate staff member. Remove the PC from the network and use the anti-virus software to disinfect the file. If this doesn't work, seek specialist support.

Exercise 9

Step 1   A firewall is a filter that determines what can pass into and out from a computer system.

Step 2   False. It should be updated at least weekly.

Step 3   You should regularly scan the computer, automatically scan e-mails and downloads from the Internet.

Step 4   It can quarantine the file.

Step 5   Anti-spam software.

Exercise 10

Step 1   a) is the best password because it contains a combination of letters and numbers and is of an adequate length.

Step 2   A user name, or log-in name.

Step 3   Access rights.

Step 4   Authentication, identification and authorisation.

Exercise 12

Step 1   A bank will never request information in this way - delete any messages like this.

Step 2   They could apply for credit or store cards, open bank accounts, obtain a driving license or passport.

Exercise 13

Step 1   Password protection should be used.

Step 2   Never share a password or PIN, never write it down, change it regularly.

Step 3   Authentication is the process a computer uses to find out if someone is who they say they are.

Step 4   The authorisation process checks your access permissions.

Step 5   You should change your password or PIN regularly.

Step 6   Phishing.

Step 7   Identity theft.

Exercise 14

Step 1   Cables can be used to lock IT equipment to office furniture.

Step 2   Because of their size and portability.

Exercise 15

Step 1   To make sure you have a copy, in case files are deleted accidentally, data becomes corrupted, the computer malfunctions or is lost totally.

Step 2   Backed up data should be kept off site.

Step 3   Yes. You should do some backing up of files.

Step 4   Software media should be stored securely, away from any risk of damage or theft.

Exercise 16

Step 1   A public network is vulnerable because computers on it are visible to computers outside the network.

Step 2   Wireless networks must be secured to prevent outside access.

Step 3   Encryption is the process of scrambling data into a form that can't be understood by unauthorised persons.

Step 4   Bluetooth connectivity is wireless and automatic.

Exercise 18

Step 1   Backing up.

Step 2   Hourly, daily, weekly, or whenever necessary.

Step 3   Backup media should be kept in a storage environment that is theft-proof, waterproof and fireproof.

Step 4   A network.

Step 5   Computers on a public network can be seen by computers outside the network; those on a private network cannot.

Step 6   Bluetooth connectivity connects various devices automatically.

Step 7   No. You should always use your own password for security reasons.

Glossary

Adware	Software that causes adverts to pop up or be downloaded.
Application	A stand-alone piece of software which can be used for a specific purpose.
Anti-spam software	Protects the computer from receiving known spam messages.
Anti-virus software	Protects the computer from virus threats.
Backing up	Making copies of all important files.
Bluetooth	Wireless connectivity, allows you to connect multiple devices.
Computer Virus	A malicious piece of code which can cause damage to computerised systems.
Control Panel	An area on the computer from which the user can perform advanced administrative tasks.
Encryption	Scrambling of information to make it difficult to understand.
Firewall	A filter to control traffic from your PC to the Internet and vice versa.
Hacker	Someone who changes software from its intended use and can infiltrate a computer system.
Hardware	Any physical part of a computer system.
Hoax e-mail	Chain letters, etc. intended to cause nuisance or harm or obtain personal information.
Identity theft	Stealing personal information to use for fraudulent means.
Password	A secret combination of letters and numbers used when logging on.
Phishing	The practice of trying to obtain personal information by pretending to be a legitimate organisation.
Privacy policy	Rules held by an organisation to govern the use of sensitive and confidential information.
Rogue dialler	Software that causes dial up connections to dial premium rate numbers rather than the correct ISP number.
Spam	Junk e-mail messages.
Spyware	Software installed without a user's knowledge that interferes with their use of the computer.
Trojan	Software that masquerades as something else in order to gain access to a computer.
User name	Used to log on to a computer.
Worm	Software that creates copies of itself and spreads through a network.

Index

Record of Achievement Matrix

This Matrix is to be used to measure your progress while working through the guide. This is a learning reinforcement process, you judge when you are competent.

Tick boxes are provided for each feature. 1 is for no knowledge, 2 some knowledge and 3 is for competent. A section is only complete when column 3 is completed for all parts of the section.

Tick the Relevant Boxes **1**: No Knowledge   **2**: Some Knowledge   **3**: Competent

Section	No.	Driving Lesson	1	2	3
1 Security Awareness	1	Awareness			
	2	E-mail Basics			
	3	Unwanted and Hoax Messages			
	4	Viruses			
	5	Other Threats			
2 Protecting your PC	7	Anti-virus Measures			
	8	Anti-virus Software			
3 Information Security	10	Privacy Issues			
	11	Changing a Password			
	12	Information Security			
4 Technology Security	14	Physical Measures			
	15	Keeping Data Safe			
	16	Network and Wireless Security			
	17	Passwords and Security Settings			

Other Products from CiA Training Ltd

CiA Training Ltd is a leading publishing company, which has consistently delivered the highest quality products since 1985. A wide range of flexible and easy to use self teach resources has been developed by CiA's experienced publishing team to aid the learning process. These include the following related products at the time of publication of this product:

- **BCS Improving Productivity using IT**

- **ECDL/ICDL Syllabus 5.0**

- **ECDL/ICDL Advanced Syllabus 2.0**

- **ECDL/ICDL Revision Series**

- **ECDL/ICDL Advanced Syllabus 2.0 Revision Series**

Previous syllabus versions also available - contact us for further details.

We hope you have enjoyed using our materials and would love to hear your opinions about them. If you'd like to give us some feedback, please go to:

www.ciatraining.co.uk/feedback.php

and let us know what you think.

New products are constantly being developed. For up to the minute information on our products, to view our full range, to find out more, or to be added to our mailing list, visit:

www.ciatraining.co.uk